Words

Into Life

Jessica Eady

PUBLISHED by PARABLES
Earthly Stories with a Heavenly Meaning

Words

Into Life

Jessica Eady

PUBLISHED by PARABLES
Earthly Stories with a Heavenly Meaning

About The Book

Words into Life was created as a diverse set of poetry relating to life experiences, the finding of spirituality, and the beginning of healing through the expression of words. I desire all walks of life to feel connected and not alone. Often we experience disappointment, heartaches, and punch to the gut trials that sometimes leave us feeling isolated. I long to provide a haven if you will, for the hurting, misunderstood, lonely, or un-encouraged reader. Poetic words can heal, relate and inspire. Words Into Life, in hopes, will help connect and encourage humanity to move forward knowing circumstance never seizes greatness! I hope you as the reader tap into your greater awareness and deepest parts of your being un-hindered, soaring into the greater heights of life. There is freedom. There is more. There is hope.

About The Author

Author Jessica Eady, age 30 and single mother of a beautiful little girl named Lily. Just short of 3 years ago my family underwent a traumatic divorce that brought battles and trials I never knew existed. Wars with darkness, sorrow, grief, and tremendous pain. Pain that tried to hold us in a prison. I had to re-program, renew thought capacities from years of emotional/physical abuse. I had to rediscover parts of identity and build life from the ground up. Words into Life was birthed through a season of regaining freedom and trying to rediscover faith. Through the pressure of frustration and the forging of my journey I was able to find hope, search out who God really was and see who I truly am. Whatever circumstances we find ourselves in, may our lives carve a story throughout the pathways of life. Producing a VOICE in us no one can silence! Regaining strength. Claiming OUR words into life!

Blazing Staircases of Fire.

Blazing staircases of fire
And distant memories I no longer desire
Uncorked screws and   gentle barbed wire
Unmarked gems and hidden sapphires
The indwelling of keys...
I begin to reach new corridors and see
Deep within, I know the past places can't find me
I suddenly...
Reach that high place where I'm above them all
No longer held against these walls
Like a little child and her baby doll
So tender and intertwined with life's questions and blurred lines
This unknowing light
It's of a Savior that began to blind
Me.
Continued On Next Page

As if it's the one key Fantasy or reality?
I gaze for a minute...
A Known or unknown place...
A starving space
Of imaginary arms of smothering grace that
unlocked the masks of my hidden face
I began to taste
The sweet notions of this slow pace
Lover of my soul
The staircase....l'm walking...My new, safe place.

Stardust eyes.

Midnight stars parade my galaxy like indigo embers of the night
My identity began to leap deep inside the vast inner core of mine
I know that I can never disappear from this knowing
Of what I am inside

Everything begins to silence the wrath of the shadows of my past
and I am home again
The thin layers of heaven...

The intricate creatures of Cherubim...
The ancient gates that sing to me
The glass crown that waits for me...

I'm the bride of this majesty
The lover adorned by gracious infinity
Divinity, it longs for me...

Oh light of morning, I wish you not to come
So that the mystery of this night is sung by songs of finding
The winding of my childhood music box and grinding of the
unopened hidden locks of this space
I wait...
Continued On Next Page

There's more beyond these stars of vintage kryptonite
It's the depth of awakened life
Between this space and time, carries the Door that longs for me
I open.
I sit inside thee.
I match eyesight.
Blood type.
Everything.
My God, this knowing I finally found my creator.

Inheritance.

Peace she writes
Anguish she divides
Within her hands she creates currencies of life
Moments of purpose she rides
Inspire
Throws fire
Rewired
Hardwired she became, a rebirth of light
An awaiting bride, transformed into a royal wife
Of covenant
A summit, of Lion roars
Longing for more....
Now, Never the same
She grabs hold of her Lion mane renamed
She inherits His all
Falling into His holy arms of mercy ransomed
A sacred baby-doll
A poet of His love
More than Enough.

The Injustice

We weather the storms we weather the wages

We pave black tops with hearts and keep them in cages.
We run free on golden lit pathways only finding that we're only
halfway...

In dreams we ween towards what we once thought we loved.
Where we find mystical doves and fantasies of promises we
thought we wouldn't become.
We built platforms and stages for ourselves in ways are
dangerous...

We looked above for all our questions that aren't filled with our
sugar coated sessions.
Then we find, in our fine dined settings all that we lost
We then notice our costs, eyes once covered in swamp embedded
moss.

We picture the loss...
We soon began to hold on to what wasn't ours, and lost countless
hours...
Continued On Next Page

Became cowards and let go grip.
We took sips of humility then; And because of what life upruptly
enforced
We signed our names on all that was endorsed

We let it go
We said no
We embraced
Face to face we became
Searching for a new name
Game over to the mundane
Push over, reclaim. Move over, fast lane!

A Dream.

I waged a war a thousand times.
I kept a fight without any signs.
I used every line I could asking God if he just would.

I searched above then looked beyond.
Wishing on stars and majestic wands
I hold my breath.
With this still, vacant feeling of death
To a passion...

A ration of hope I grasp, from the poverty of some self- stricken
mask of a dream.
Someone wake me with a meaning.
Somewhere deep with embers gleaming.
I'll cross another desert...

I'll hold up this heart that's bleeding...
Oh guardian, hold fast this hand, and keep me not from the
dreaming
I want to fly.
Continued On Next Page

I won't sit on this barren land and die.
Will you lie with me?
Show me where to abide? I won't hide
I'll run with chariots of heaven along this pierced and broken
side.

Lover's heart and stricken eyes. I will know my place and sigh
Quelling comfort of life alive
As others soon find… a soul redefined
An ancient key of dross, I unlocked free, Oh sweet liberate
Liberate me.

Soul Journey

In a world of purple skies and sweet amber lullabies…

I wait
Here in my mind of thoughtful journeys and daring rides
Of countless thoughts and choosing sides
Attending to this imagination of self-created lines
These boundaries I hide behind...
Clarity, vitality, certainty, imagery...
All would be lost if I chose otherwise
But you see. . .
Deep down in the inner core of me
There lies a human being
Founded on the mind far beyond seeing
Desiring love, worth, and value
Away from a population that desperately wants to sell you
Are we all not just a life?
Searching for a purpose that we know feels right
Oh the longing…
The burning calling beneath our feet
We hurt and ignore that divine meet
No longer shall we wait.

Mystery of the Woods

You're like the lurking shadow behind the trees of the woods
of my life
Your presence is there yet I can't define you
It startles me, but at least I know somewhere deep within
these trees you're there
I walk along this moonlight of every night hour,
yet still loves leaves this sour longing
I'm a wayward soul
I'm a lover abound

Where amongst this sound of the woods'
smell linger will I find you
Anew
Quick my stars, they turned blue
Wooing me across the ebony trees of the new
There beneath me..
I sank deep.

My heart awakening from its sleep
You're my mystery.
Divine.
Continued On Next Page

Away from the familiar signs and past lullabies
A wander of this night
A lantern of light
Hands holding onto for sweet dear life...
Now, but the sound, is only my feet brushed against the harkened
leaves and grass where they both meet
Suddenly...
The lies inside go dim
Suddenly.. .1 discover Him
More and more, within.
Father I whisper
Seraphim

Tongue speaks

Vast, honest than most
I thought it was my good until it became my worst
I couldn't divide the violence of my tongue
So used to losing, this time... I thought I won

The tongue
Of a violent sword it was
Twisted, manifested opinions... it does what it does
Nevertheless
It wouldn't if we understood love
Therefore boundaries at stake
Break ground..
Confound me
Surround me

I voice, I'll no longer hold me in this prison
No longer prohibit the divine vision
Of our lives under sacred circumcision

Bridle the tongue
So that therefore it speaks only sounds of purified doves
In the air
Continued On Next Page

I began to care again
Hues of warmth touched my voice again
Running down liquid of redemption
The crisp air of salvation swayed my words without former
tension
The tongue speaks with its unhidden freedom
I am a voice

Would your love...

Would your love over spill in my thoughts?
Will it create what laid dormant before?
Would your love test the theory of my own darkness?
Would it slay all the things my sword cannot?
Would your love bear arms against
the wicked in front of me,
undergoing the blind spots of spiritual sight
left in desolation...

I can no longer be up against these things alone....

As I whisper to my maker I ask one thing, if love endures,
where is your love now?

Not in the slightest doubting ... but here's my honest
questioning that lays naked before you....

Beneath Trees

I find myself beneath the trees
Where lilies grow along side of me
And Spanish moss hangs from my past keys
I want to gaze at the sky from the ground
And know my hurts wear a crown.
I don't want to learn from bias kings of the Earth
I want truth, I want girth of what's real
I want to feel
What life's like
To be surreal
I hate that moments are still…
Still beneath the trees of contending
I desire the movement now, but I know I'm learning me
To see, from a place on high instead of beneath
Where lovers of my soul meet
Concrete run upon my seat
Beneath this crimson shade of a tree
I ponder life
Unlocking the more inside of me

Little Girl Little Girl

I'm like a little girl in the quaking corner
shaking with her teddy bear.
Waiting for my maker to sing me a new song.
I can hear the rhythmic beat from afar
I can almost hear the lyrics piercing my heart
The distance seems so far from where I'm sitting, to the
DOOR

I can feel his thunder up from beneath me
The fire from his eye giving my room warmth...
The sacred part of me that thinks it's so dark,
Starts to see it's His eternal Glory

I get up and begin to walk
An ember then sparks
It's the core of his chest as a lit flame
Igniting all my darkness

A pair of wings began to grow from behind me
For the first time they didn't need to be hidden
Continue On Next Page

The Sound of my Song
grew louder and became even closer
I knew it was Him

I came to the door labeled BEHOLD
I asked, would you receive me"?
This odd, peculiar like thing?
What would happen if I knocked?
Mystery then filled my space

Love ponders

Would you hold someone? Love someone?
Go out of the way for someone
Would you

Would you lean? Glean from someone?
Reach someone
Teach someone
Be cool and pure with someone?
Embrace and stand for someone?
Believe in someone
Retrieve someone
Bend and break the flesh of someone
Catch someone?
Rest with someone
Die and give your last breath for someone?

Love
It's the purpose of our human race
To reach the faces of society with gentleness.
It isn't relational infatuation. Instead...
It's the punctuation of our life line.
Our sublime
Continued On Next Page

Opposing the toxic time of dimes
That buy us useless rhymes of fake love songs.
It isn't a bias love story of the earth.

We are the dirt made of clay
Air in the lungs
Youth hearts young
So Alive our veins thrive
Let us live another day in the eyes of what
Passion sighs
And be free.

See.
With the heart instead of the mind
Rewind. The days to go slower
To catch up with the days that caused you to bend lower
Remain...
Until one day you to choose to love again

Silence

Silence is the airwaves of our being
If we listen closely, we can hear our soul singing
It's not in the violent scream; instead it's in the whisper
Where mountain heights and evergreens are sisters
We can't miss her
It's the silence
The vibrant peace in life
Where we may or we might
Fly flight of a wind breeze glimpse of a night
Oh lover of absent noise gone white
Here we can lay
Here we can drif by day
Sweet, sweet silence mother may,
Hold onto you forever
Sweet, sweet silence never
To clever to stay
I'll remember you this way

Square peg

I try to squeeze myself in a round hole.
But I lose my senses.
My spiritual senses. I can't hear, I can't see
Maybe because I'm not being me.

I lose peace, I can't see anything around me.
Everything. Inside goes blind.
I'm frantic, lost, and living outside
Of touch where I can feel life.

So tired of squeezing..... forcing.... Living on means of what's
taught as "right"
I can't find
The light to the path
The match
The something that pulls on me from the inside

Outside, outsider
Divider
Striver
Make me the passenger and no longer the driver
Make me wiser
Continued On Next Page

I'm tired
Made from a different hard wire
Rider
Of the waves
I'm not afraid
Find the place in which I'm made
For.

Open doors and eccentric worlds
They Curl, me into the crease
Of everything that screams
Divinity
Sing to me, the songs that pave the way.

We Are

We are the light of the world.
A story untold.
A mystic force un-controlled.
A violent love of magnetic, poetic molds.

We are the light of the world.
Of truth and Love.
Blessed in the fields and blessed in the cities above.
We are armed forces of saints and light.
Angelic humans of wars and fights that takes us back to
heights in which we were made for.

Others alike.
We differ from the planes of our realities.
The formulated keys of our inheritance
Made for more than the night hours we struggle in.

Till then...
I cuddle within the crease of my maker...
Singing songs of my already created future.

Mindful Mind

If today would go by as a thousand years in my eyes
I'd learn something
I'd learn as the days die and my ways pass by,
burning themselves in shores along genocide
I would no longer poison myself
with the introspection of self- inspection
Where passions created a divided section
Rations inside the world of a mind made free

Dark enchanted, waves of a sea
Sudden blackened signs and colorblind
Someone lift this fog of sublime
Oh, dear God
Save this wretched soul of mine
Lifting these eyes to a new place of DIVINE
I'M DESPERATE
I'M SEARCHING
Continued On Next Page

These feet are learning
Yearning
Tossing and turning with thoughts of not wanting
Bared down teeth and grunting
Woe to thee oh God I scream,
would you cause such cup to pass from me?
This dead horse I'm carrying... Take my hand instead,
afar off worrying
Draw me into the gate keeper's glee
Set this far off mind free Humbled Galaxy...
Of sweet hope and wonder
I ask one thing
Raise me like a father and Hold me as a mother?!
As I awaken slumber
Do not depart from me

Thoughts & Hearts & Ever-last

In these quaint thoughts of clear glass
Maybe mornings of Ever-last? I sit, awaiting times and
chimes of life to swing by me and
Hit a note I remember
Maybe a member of the heart to remind me once, of all the
lines I hit perfectly...
Could it rewind me back to a memory where complacency
wasn't complacent and sulking wasn't grieving?
Meaning! Meaning to everything that falls in front of my
face...
It about simple grace
Right? But!
This obstacle that runs circles in my heart received its
luck...
Now mornings will never be the same
I've noticed more of the meaning of my name
Refinement and its best
Turning away from selfish mess,
I'm different.
I can see
Revelation keys
Scars of burden won't remember me.
Carried mornings of mother ever- last and victory

Mind waves

In our minds are waves; vast is the sum of them.
We don't understand the current, nor the tide, but we run
from them.
We sit along our shores awaiting the safety of what's still.
Wrestling our wills and bypassing the kills of time.
Rewind.
Yet through our eyes we hold the shallow end of our zen .
Maybe trying to gain clarity again
In opposite worlds of what's in our thoughts and what's in
front of us.
Back and forth pulls of a hearts just.
Oh, the waves of our minds and the ocean of our times
Depth, mystery, feelings, roars, riddles and rhymes,
Above I watch, waiting for the sun to shine
Here's to the deep. . .
I sink into you while I wait.

Artists

They sway and move to the rhythmic beat
They understand the iconic life's bitter sweet
They shift and change into the imagery of a passionate
mind challenged by majestic idolatry
How can they be?
Without dancing to the colorful melodies that
seemingly pull them into fantasy
They desire, they love, violently.
Woe to the one that leaves behind this train of
enchanted artistic affection
Believing in the depth and meaning of a people many
would only question
They fuel life and piece the human soul together again
Things never dieing or reaching their end around them
Here's to the artists that fill the holes of what's lost
Fusing them to mend
Alas....
Golden hearts of the burning one's we ask
For.
The world waits...
Waits for you...
So Create.

Roses

Serenity of reflective Roses
Defining beauty, it cries out my name
Pleading frailty…
How could this rarity match something the same
It released life.
Marrying grace and taking names
This would suffice? I suppose.
Would it un-fold
Before my eyes so I could rewind
This moment where I lost my life
To bliss and picked it up again
To a sweet kiss of gentleness
A fragrance, a mist
Captivate me, oh place of Serenity! Rose pedals and
midnight tea
I've gone and traveled afar
Liberate me

Life dice "

Peace it overflows with rainbows and chimes of life
Ever-last to crisp air she writes...
Gratitude embedded in her rights
There she goes, she rolls her dice
She blew a vengeance kiss to her old friend strife
Once a wife. . .Now a rifle
This girl laughs at the top of the Eiffel
Tower.
Could this be freedom or power?
Of the girl who stands in a divine hour
Rubber meeting her road
Out from the rain and cold
She sold her past to the darkness that once kept it
Running toward her Father where she would forever sit
Under a savoring love that drips
This.
This was her moment.
This is where she grabbed her life
This is where she threw the dice.
Game over she rides…
Into the new day that broke forth light

Mirror of a man

A man meets his reflection
Drawing him into his sacred redemption
He studies the lines in his face
Meeting his first real moments of grace
He then is taken back to those places
The places of Real
With a strong heart and a burning Zeal
He finally, looks himself in the eye
With a sigh of relief he is alive
Now knowing the hands that rests gently upon him
His scared light cannot dim
Because of this place he recently finds as his own
This place of rest
Within himself he calls his home
Identity known
Shalom.

Is this the end?

The end that I was so quickly brought to by you.
My once beginning, that you knew
My pure white gown now turned to blue...
Such frayed chapters and distant memories now
Our two worlds came crashing down...
I sigh
The divide
You took my hand; and made a plan
You circled your whole created life in mine...
You signed away your name and I handed you mine..
Memorized by the day I found you...
My beginning . . . what did we do?
At last
I free my soul from what I thought I knew
Forgiving the sorrowful thought of you
Laying down credit, where credit is due
I dispose the toxicity of this season's blues
Woe, now, to breathe in deep
I sway to this new colorful beat of life and how it moves
me into something different
I inhabit the suspense

Sacred Place

I'm just trying to find that sacred place inside of me.
Where I used to meet with holy perspectives and see.
Are my depths to deep?
Are they stale?
Are the colors of my vitality frail?
Should I need to die all over again to find you?
Rewind you...
Through gardens of cloves
Remold .
Wherever that mystic strength resides, I want to travel there
Where a sorrow- filled book of a soul would dare
To search the canvas of abstract, self- sought whys and
cares
Desired flutes and lyres,
Cry out I pause,
Drink of the moment and think

I will journey out again to find you

Love Alike

Eyes of love, burn like fire.
Fury of the night's day.
Flickered flame, you light the way to a lover's heart astray.
Singing songs of a mystery blue-jay...
As you wait, I wait.
Cement clouds dissipate.
I won't hesitate.
I will love again.

PUBLISHED *by* PARABLES
Earthly Stories with a Heavenly Meaning

CPSIA information can be obtained
at www.ICGtesting.com
Printed in the USA
BVHW060806100319
542244BV00027B/790/P